To Paula Williams

Thanks so much for all you do to help heal people with their heart issues.

You are beautiful

Monica Dogle Das

God Made Me Beautiful, But I Didn't Know It

by
Monica Douglas Davis

authorHOUSE®

AuthorHouse™
1663 Liberty Drive, Suite 200
Bloomington, IN 47403
www.authorhouse.com
Phone: 1-800-839-8640

© 2007 Monica Douglas Davis. All rights reserved.

No part of this book may be reproduced, stored in a retrieval system, or transmitted by any means without the written permission of the author.

First published by AuthorHouse 12/13/2007

ISBN: 978-1-4343-3354-4 (sc)

Printed in the United States of America
Bloomington, Indiana

This book is printed on acid-free paper.

Acknowledgements

I would like to thank God for allowing me the opportunity to write this book. I truly believe that it is my destiny to write this book and to have the things in my life to bring me to the point to write it. I believe in divine destiny.

I thank my spiritual leaders Bishop Gary Hawkins and Elder Debbie Hawkins, from Voices of Faith, for showing me what faith can do. I am a woman of faith and your leadership and examples of faith inspire me to dream big and to reach high in exercising my faith. You both love your congregation and you practice what you preach.

Elder Barbara Jones, you inspire me to work towards my goals as you work on your own to help families have better lives.

To the large group of people I call friends, I am grateful that I have had the privilege to know each of you.

To Elihu and Mary Cook, you have been my friends for many years. I love you both for always accepting me in your lives.

Jeff, Lorraine, Neadie, Tee, Lori, Sheri, Anthonio, Theresa, Carla, Delisha, Candace, Shamika, Trina, Gay, Jennifer, Tamera, Dr. Shelton and all the Gwinnett Rockdale Newton Community Service Board staff who work so hard and are underpaid, you help people in many ways. It was a pleasure working with all of you.

To the people I worked with at Babies Can't Wait in Dekalb County, you work with infants and toddlers at a critical period in their lives. It was a privilege working with you. Special thanks to Myrna, Nancy, Nisey, Phillip, Yvette, Mudiwa, and Ron. Keep up the great work.

To the entire former teacher co-workers, principals, staff members and everyone who helped run the schools I worked at, including the lunch attendants and janitorial staff, you are also all special people. Often we get so much from our teachers and I want you to know that it makes a real difference in your students' lives. Remember to speak positive words to the young people because their future, in part, is determined from what they hear from you.

A special thanks to Marva Walker, my mentor during my time at Lawndale Academy. You truly helped me learn about teaching and you've been teaching for over 35 years now.

To the hundreds of students and clients I worked with over the past 14 years, you are all special and beautiful. You have choices to make in life. Choose the ones that will benefit your life. Remember, I always said, "You can do it. All you have to do is put your mind to it and do it. I encourage you to choose to do good things."

To my children that I have worked with that had special needs; you are all unique and valuable people. The world needs your gift. Find out what your gift is and use it to benefit society. Don't allow yourself to be negatively labeled or restricted because of your disability. Your disability is only a small part of who you are and many times they can be overcome with your hard work. Look at examples of great people with disabilities that have impacted the world. Many artists, musicians, athletes and professional people had disabilities but they rose to great levels. Some examples are Stevie Wonder, Ray Charles, Althea Gibson, Carl Brashear, Helen Keller and many others.

To all of the people who give of their time and talent to volunteer to help others that I have worked with over the years, your contribution to society doesn't go unnoticed. I truly love all of you in a special way.

To my friend Valerie Hawkins, who I have known since high school, and Valerie Rocchild, who I worked with at Castrol Industrial, you are both special women. I value our long-term friendships.

To the women from my former book club, The Ladies of Literature: Ruby, Pat, Terry, Dolly, Katrina, Peaches, Denise, Margarite, and Stacey, I hope you read and enjoy this book.

To Kelly Shipp, Jennifer Kapner and Laila, I enjoy our walks in the park and talks about motherhood. We are all learning together and I can't wait to see what the future has in store for our children.

To my other friends I don't always see or talk to often, you are always in my thoughts: Angie Starks, Felicia and William Cole, Shelia and Glenn Hayes, Mike and Daphne Garrett, Terry Odell, David and Lynn King, Ramona Davison, Dora Williams, Terry Nelder, Marlene Leon, Patrice Johnifer Brown, Noelize Hilaire, Joyce Perkins, Angela Thomas, Angela Austin, Juanita Sprull, Audrey Payne, Carol Wilby, Rhonda Fulgham and Tina Curry, I hope you know how special you are to me.

To Ronald Harris, I am so proud of you. You have one more year of high school to finish. Finish with pride and hard work. I can't wait to see what your future holds. Thank your mother Angie Starks, for raising you to be the great young man you are.

To Lois McLain, Cleo Browder, Marie Crayton and Dierdre Neeley, we met in graduate school and have maintained our friendships. I hope you know how great a contribution your counseling work is to society. I look forward to hearing about your success in a noble and often unappreciated field. Keep up the good work.

To all of my nieces and nephews, I hope you know that your aunt loves you dearly, even though I don't see you often. I enjoy our visits and look forward to seeing what great things your future holds.

To all of my family members in Memphis, and St. Louis, it seems like we only see each other at weddings and funerals, but we are family and I do love you all. We should have a family reunion soon.

To my two sisters-in-laws Alicia and Talonda Douglas, you are both great mothers and I hope we can become closer as time passes.

To my new family through my marriage, Marcus, Bonnie, Serita, Aishah, Adjoa, Chris, Dedan, Timothy, Valerie, Shariee, Soweto, Nandi, Abena, Loretta, Veronica, Abena and Bosia, I hope we become a true family over time since my own family lives in Chicago and Toledo. Special thanks to Bosia, my father-in-law, for restoring my childhood picture for the book cover.

To my husband, Kweku, and son, Isaiah, you are an answer to my prayers. I want you to know how much I love you and pray that you will always know how special and how beautiful you are to me.

To all the people who read this book, I want you to know that you are truly special and you were created with a purpose. I hope this book lets you know that God made us all beautiful!

Introduction

This idea came to me on February 25, 2007, as I thought about what my purpose in life is and how I want to be a positive influence on young people. Oprah Winfrey opened a school in South Africa this year for girls who will become potential leaders. I watched the show and it brought tears to my eyes. I wanted to do my part. I have complained about things in my life that I am unhappy about, but those circumstances seem so insignificant compared to what so many of the young girls have faced.

    I grew up in the inner city of Chicago, Illinois, on the west side of the city. My family consisted of two parents and eight children. I am the second oldest child, and the oldest girl. We were sometimes called the black "eight is enough" family. There are four girls and four boys. My father always worked and my mother stayed home with the children. I never felt like we were in need of anything material because I went to a private school and took piano lessons for nine years and band lessons when I went to high school. We never had designer clothes, but we were always clean. People gave us things and we had several cars, although not all of them ran. None of our neighbors had as much as my family did in my eyes, so I thought we were doing well.

As a child I always had short hair. Growing up in the '70s, hair was a big deal, as well as the color of your skin. I had short hair and dark skin, so I was considered unattractive and even ugly to some people. I remember being called ugly for three years straight because of the length of my hair. I compared my hair to the girl in my class that had the shortest hair next to mine. I tried to prove that my hair was longer by pulling it to show my classmates. I almost got into a fight with the other girl because she had to prove that her hair was longer than mine.

It still is an issue I deal with almost 40 years later. I have not left my house sometimes, if I didn't like my hair. When I was a teenager I wore a carefree curl. It really made my hair grow. I believe it was the daily moisturizer that stimulated the hair growth. I ruined many shirts and blouses with the curl spray and left stains on furniture. It really is funny now thinking about it, but back then, it was a style.

My father was and still is a humorous man, but he wasn't affectionate. My parents never told me I was beautiful, attractive or even loved and I looked for that love outside of my home. I truly believe that my parents did love me, but they never verbally said it when I was growing up. It was implied by their actions, but as a child, I needed to hear the words.

I became very insecure, felt unlovable and unattractive, so I put myself in some dangerous situations when I was a teenager. I have gotten into a car with a strange man because he said I was pretty. I am thankful to God to this day that he didn't hurt me. He did make his intentions known to me, but I asked him to take me home and he did. I was very fortunate.

I was also very vulnerable and naïve. When I was in high school, I was conned by some adults. It was called the pigeon drop. I ended up losing two coats I had just gotten out of layaway and $30.

I have been involved in dating situations and relationships that were unhealthy to be in during my adolescence and early adulthood. I am grateful to be alive.

The reason I am writing this book is to hopefully encourage all people, but specifically women, to see that they are all beautiful no matter what they look like physically, or what experiences they have had in their lives. I hope the words of this book will impact women, both young and old, to know how valuable they are and how they are truly beautiful and special.

Ten years or so ago, Karen Murray, a friend of mine, was talking about life and growing up insecure. Karen came up with the title of this book and I said we would write it together. I have lost touch with Karen, but I believe the message of this book is needed. I am now a mother and on February 28, 2007, at 2:00AM, I was looking at my five-month-old son's face and the words for this book came to me. As I look into my son's face, I see my eyes. Of course, I think he is so beautiful, and the thought came to me, if he's beautiful, I must be, too.

GOD MADE ME BEAUTIFUL! It has taken me almost 40 years to finally believe this. Beauty begins on the inside and we must all learn how to find our inner beauty to bring us strength as we travel through this journey called life. Beauty isn't only a superficial, outward societal based standard of your appearance. Beauty is the source that drives you to be authentic and persevere in life no matter what obstacles you encounter. Beauty is the drive to succeed and accept yourself as a lovable, capable person in this world with a purpose. Beauty is what draws others to you. It is an attitude knowing that you are a unique and special person that no one else can duplicate.

If I can leave one message with people as they read this book, the message is: You are beautiful because God made you and everything God makes is good. Beauty is a spirit deep within that says: I am Here, and my life does matter. I love you all.

I Am Beautiful

When God formed us, he placed beauty in all of us. He chose the color of our eyes, skin and texture of our hair. He decided the physical limitations we would have or even diseases or disabilities we would be born with before we were ever birthed into this world. We were fearfully and wonderfully created in our mothers' wombs. Every person is unique. Even identical twins aren't truly identical. They have their own personality and character.

Whether I was created in an act of lust or love, I am beautiful. It doesn't matter if I was born to a couple, or a single mom. I am beautiful. Was I raised by my mother, grandmother, two parents, father, foster parents or in an orphanage? I am beautiful. I was, I am, and I will always be beautiful. God made me beautiful, but I didn't know it.

If I was raised in the ghettos of the inner city, on a farm, or in Suburbia, I am beautiful. Do I know the sounds of happiness and laughter of children playing, or am I familiar with the cries of hunger, sadness, fear, abuse, or neglect? I am beautiful. Was I raised in poverty or privilege? Have I ever been in need? Did I eat with government assistance or was I served by others? Did I live on the streets and eat whatever I could find or was offered to me? Was my primary care giver employed, a stay at home mom, a teenager, self- employed, or did I benefit from my grandparents or some other relative's inheritance? I am beautiful. Was I exposed to drugs, gangs, and violence? Maybe my childhood was scarred by sexual, physical and/or mental abuse. Was I afraid to come home, or afraid to go to school? Was I homeless, living in shelters, abandoned buildings, cars or on the streets? I am beautiful.

Was I an only child, a result of a multiple birth, or one of many siblings? I am beautiful. I was, I am, and I will always be beautiful. God made me beautiful, but I didn't know it.

Was I a product of mixing races? Did my parents come from different cultures or social status? I am beautiful. Was I teased, ridiculed, mocked, or made fun of because I was told I was mixed up and didn't fit in? I am beautiful. Was I picked on because of my appearance, the way I dressed, talked, smelled, or walked? I am beautiful. Was my disability the talk of many people that said mean or negative things behind my back or directly to my face? Was I picked on or isolated and teased because I was "different from other people?" I am beautiful. I was, I am, and I will always be beautiful. God made me beautiful, but I didn't know it.

God Made Me Beautiful, But I Didn't Know It

Before I ever heard a harsh, mean, or negative word, I was beautiful. After I learned that words can cut you worse than a knife, I am beautiful. Tall, thin, lite, four eyed, skinny, fat, black, ugly, nappy headed, bald headed, miss goody two shoes, nerd, good girl, freak, stupid, ignorant, good for nothing, unwanted and even hated. I am still beautiful.

Short hair, straight hair, stringy hair, curly hair or bald, I am beautiful. Before I ever thought of cutting, coloring, straightening, perming, lightening, weaving, putting in waves, braids, or extensions in my hair, I am beautiful. I was, I am, and I will always be beautiful. God made me beautiful, but I didn't know it.

Did I excel in school, or lag behind? Did I barely make it through school and graduate? Did I have to repeat a grade or two? Did I drop out? Whatever the situation was, I am beautiful.

Prior to being called honey, baby, girl, sweetie, whore or other derogatory, degrading words, I was beautiful. After being whistled at, touched, fondled, pinched, prodded, poked, handled, grabbed, harassed, molested, beaten or raped, I am still beautiful. If I learned to be afraid, insecure, unloved, isolated, deflated, disgraced, disrespected, untrusting of others and of myself, I am beautiful. I was, I am, and I will always be beautiful. God made me beautiful, but I didn't know it.

As I grew older and experienced the hurts of life like death, disease, disappointment, poverty, devastation, divorce and dismay. I am still beautiful. Have I experienced joy, love, hope, peace, kindness, patience and perseverance as I interacted with others, family and friends, co-workers, and community? I am beautiful.

Whether I believed in myself, or the words others said to me, both helpful or hurtful. I am still beautiful. I was, I am, and I will always be beautiful. God made me beautiful, but I didn't know it.

Am I a barren woman, or a mother of one child or more? Did I carry children in my womb that were never born or died early in their lives? Was I a mother through adoption, or foster care, a big sister, a mentor, a surrogate mother or a mother through volunteer efforts? I am beautiful. Did I raise my children through adulthood or let the world raise them while I was in search of myself? Even through the pain of addiction, compulsion, mental or physical illness, and over indulgence, I am still beautiful. My inner person may have been crying out for help, guidance and deliverance, and my actions were not beautiful, but my heart still had beauty in it. As I search for self-fulfillment, security, self-esteem, success, and the significance of life, I am beautiful. Through tears, trials, tests, temptations, and tribulations that have come my way, I am still beautiful. I was, I am, and I will always be beautiful. God made me beautiful, but I didn't know it.

Will I become a teacher, or leader, or will I be a follower in the crowd? Will I find a cure for some disease, make the world a safer place to live, set policy and make laws to govern the people? Will I stand for what I believe is right or will I sit back and accept what is given to me? Will I become a victim of ignorance, fear, prejudice, or violence, or become a prisoner inside of myself because I don't know what I believe? Will I soar like an eagle high in the sky rising to heights few people have seen? Will I search deep inside myself to find that inner beauty that was placed in me before I was born and set goals for myself and never give up trying until I succeed in achieving my goals? I am beautiful. I was, I am, and I will always be beautiful. God made me beautiful, but I didn't know it.

Am I a helper of others? Do I share my gifts, talents, time, and treasures with others, or do I spend my life pushing over and hurting people to get what I want and feel I deserve? Are my actions frequently offensive, mean, cruel and insensitive towards others? Do I hurt other people because I am hurt inside and don't believe or feel like I am a lovable and worthy person? Let me tell you that you were, you are, and you will be beautiful if you look for it. God made you beautiful. Believe it and others will see it also!

Can you look in the mirror and smile at the face looking back at you, or are you dissatisfied, considering surgery, not eating, taking laxatives, making yourself vomit, to look a certain way you feel society wants you to look? Do you exercise excessively or limit what you eat in an unhealthy manner? Does the mirror play tricks on you telling you that you're not beautiful? Can you look at your face for even two minutes or do you only glance briefly at the person in front of the mirror? Have you cried many days because someone told you that you need to look different from the current way that you do? You are beautiful no matter what your physical dimensions are. Repeat this affirmation ten times a day in front of the mirror every morning and evening. "I was, I am, and

I will always be beautiful. God made me beautiful." I want you to know it!

As I age and my body changes from childhood, adolescence and young adulthood, I am beautiful. I may be bigger, smaller, taller, wider, more or less developed than my peers, I am still beautiful. Even with more weight, multiple diets, abusing my body with potions, lotions, diets, pills and fads, I am beautiful. Having cosmetic surgery, physical fitness routines, positive thinking, interventions, meditation, redirections, rehabilitation, and counseling, I am beautiful. If the choices I made resulted in imprisonment, probation, parole, and/or community service, I am beautiful. While working on my actions, addictions, and attitudes, I am beautiful. If I had a nervous breakdown or suffer from mental illness and/or alcohol and drug abuse, I am still beautiful. I was, I am, and I will always be beautiful. God made me beautiful, but I didn't know it.

As I develop scars, molds, wrinkles and age spots of time, I am beautiful. During the time of life when my body loses some of its smoothness, elasticity, firmness, sheen and gravity changes, I am beautiful. When my face looks like the face of my mother, grandmother, or some other relative, I am beautiful.

Did I live my life following the advice and wishes of others, or did I make decisions on my own? Was I a people pleaser or was I a domineering, opinionated, stubborn, prideful, or just strong-willed person? Did I set goals for myself, have dreams that I pursued, or was I a wishful thinker and watcher of others? If the words careful, cautious, conscientious, conservative, play it safe, don't rock the boat, are descriptions of my character, I am beautiful. I was, I am, and I will always be beautiful. God made me beautiful, but I didn't know it.

The world is made of all kinds of people and each person has a choice to find their place in it despite the circumstances they are faced with. Beauty will always seek to elevate itself above circumstances if you let it.

Will I spend my final days in peace and comfort? Will I live a long life and die in my old age, or will my life prematurely end through some tragedy, accident, or illness? The answer is still unknown to man. Have I given to society in a positive way? Have my feet left footprints in the sand for others to follow with pride? Did my beauty shine for the world to see? Did I reach my potential or did I live life never stepping outside of my comfort zone? Did my beauty positively affect the lives of others? The choice is up to me. I was, I am, and I will always be beautiful. God made me beautiful and NOW YOU KNOW IT! What will you do with your beauty?

Examples of the Beautiful People in My Life

Beauty has been described in a myriad of ways including skin complexion, features of the face or body type and size or some other outward appearance. These features can and do change frequently.

Some days we can all look at ourselves and say, "I look good." It may be based in part on what we are wearing or what we see in the mirror, or on how we feel when we get up that day. It is a type of beauty.

Physical beauty is a part of life, but true beauty comes from the inside. There are times when I don't feel especially attractive that my husband looks at me and says, "You're beautiful!" My reaction is, "What! I have on sweats, or look at my hair. How can you think I'm beautiful when I look like this?" At that time I am basing my attractiveness on my appearance, but my husband is looking at a different type of beauty.

I'm learning to smile and say thank you to all compliments and not explain why what was said was not true. Think about it. How many times have you been complimented and you push it away with your own negative words? We can be our worse enemy or our best friend with our words.

Beauty has also been described by the type of attitude or character a person has. Your attitude is an inner reflection of yourself. It is your true essence of what makes you wonderful and unique. It also ties us in to others.

I have met many people in my life who I consider beautiful. Not because of their outward appearance, but because of their hearts.

Clarice Wimberly opened her home to me when I moved from Chicago to Atlanta. She had only met me once and I am always appreciative and grateful for her hospitality. Incidentally, she was also the person who escorted me to the hospital when my son was born. She stayed with me and held my hand when the ultrasound showed that my son had low levels of amniotic fluid and my blood pressure was high. She was and still is a great support and friend to me.

Pamela Derring, a friend I met about three years ago, has the beauty of perseverance. She's experienced many challenges since I've met her, including health issues, but her determination to continue on despite the challenges is admirable. She is outstanding and is beautiful.

Rebecca Stewart is beautiful inside and out. She has a strong will and knows what she wants and isn't willing to accept less. That truly makes her special. I believe she will be rewarded because of her strength.

My aunt, Theresa Underwood Neal, who is more like a best friend and mentor to me, has been an invaluable source of support my whole life. I've had many of my deepest and intimate conversations with her and I utilize much of her advice today.

My long time friend, Shereen Gamble, I've known since childhood. We were neighbors. She is always available for advice, laughter, and support whenever I need it. We've shared many experiences together. We went to school together, socialized, and searched for ourselves together. Through marriage and now raising children, we are still the best of friends. I know I can always count on Shereen whenever I need her.

Gloria Robinson, Shereen's mother, was always an advisor to me and I spent many hours over the years, at her house learning how to be a lady. She never let me feel like I had overstayed my welcome.

Pilara Martin has been my friend for over a decade. She listens to me when I have a problem or concern and she advises me with love while challenging my character. She expects the best for me and that makes her beautiful. She is also a personal trainer working on the outer beauty that many people are striving to achieve.

My mother, Mildred Douglas, has a quiet strong inner beauty that I struggled to understand for many years. I used to think she was weak- willed and subservient to my father, but she showed strength, courage and humility to her eight children. Her quiet and gentle spirit is a beauty that many women, actually many people, lack and find it hard to imitate. My mother made sure her children had the best education possible in the inner city of Chicago. She talked to principals about her children and enrolled my older brother and myself in the band to assist us in placement in an excellent high school. I graduated from Whitney Young Magnet High School as a result of her efforts. My mother rarely made a fuss about something, but when she did, everyone knew that it was important to her. She made sure her children spoke proper English, not street talk or slang. We were teased, but it helped me a lot. She encouraged us to do well in school. She truly is beautiful because of her humble spirit. She often puts others before herself, but she learned that she was always taken care of when she needed it.

My three younger sisters all have a beauty that's unique to them.

Mariann, has an outgoing personality and she is full of life. She is a good mother to her children and is always helping other people with their children.

Yolanda has a strong determination to succeed. She is also a single mother and she is in school part time working on her graduate degree so she can have a better life for her daughter and herself.

Sharon has a nurturing supportive type of beauty. She is a mother of four children. She is also a mortician. She is supportive of her husband and her family.

All three of my sisters are excellent mothers and they support each other frequently. They have never allowed their differences to come between them.

For years I would compare myself to my sisters and think how beautiful they were because I was always bigger in size than they were. They were raised together because they are closer in age than I was. I am six, eight and eleven years older than them, respectively. I never realized until someone told me that my sisters looked up to me and that I was an example to them. They are beautiful.

My friend, Kim Brown, has a beautiful way of supporting others. I've known Kim since college, over 20 years now, and we've had a lot of experiences in dating and relationships in common during our college years. We met when we were trying to find ourselves. Kim has helped many people find employment with her position and she has always been a source of support for me. She encourages me to go after my dreams while she also pursues her own. She has never been competitive towards me. She is genuine in her encouragement.

Renee Nolan-Muhammad, a friend who told me about a Master's degree program to become a teacher, is beautiful to me. She has a flawless complexion and a soft spoken tone. Her heart to share information has helped a great number of people. I have a Master's Degree in Education and was a teacher for eleven years because Renee was in touch with my needs and shared information with me. I tried to be a mentor as well as a teacher to my students and I always expected the best from my students. I value my friendship with Renee for over 20 years since I met her in college at The University of Illinois at Chicago. She is currently working as an assistant principal at an elementary school.

Marilyn Simpson has a deep spiritual beauty that I admire. Her love for God and desire to please him has always been one I try to emulate. We dated together and worked together and were in each others' weddings. She supported me through some of the toughest times in my life and she always had a good word for me. She never allowed me to blame myself for the mistakes other people made. She is a good friend.

Jean Teague, I call my spiritual mother. She introduced me to a deeper way to have a relationship with God. She challenged me in areas of my life that were contradictory with what I professed. Not only is her spirit beautiful, but she has a classy style of dressing. She has helped numerous women improve themselves by her example and advice.

Alicia Boyce's gift of encouragement is what I call beautiful. She is always helping someone at work, home or her church. Her generosity is admirable. She has helped people when she has faced health issues of her own. She is a hard working woman who loves others through serving.

Kathy Lewis, my quiet beautiful friend I met shortly after I moved to Georgia. She supports me and many others. She has a true gift of encouragement and service. Her words of encouragement have always made me feel special and she has also been an invaluable source of support for me. She helped me assemble exercise equipment and furniture in my house. She helps the sick and the elderly often. She is a great listener and she supports all of my dreams. She also proof reads all of the manuscripts for the books I have written.

Tonya Bowen is not only my personal beautician, but a true friend I met since I moved to Georgia. She keeps it real and tells me when I get out of line. Everyone needs at least one person who will tell them the truth about their

God Made Me Beautiful, But I Didn't Know It

flaws. She also supports me in all my endeavors. She has a deep capacity to love and serve others and strong beliefs.

Bonnie Foster, my dear mother-in-law, is beautiful for many reasons. She has a true calling to help women. Her encounter groups are discussed frequently at family gatherings. I haven't yet personally experienced one of her women's groups, but I am anxious to attend one. She is a mother figure to many people. I call her the "we are the world mother." She loves deeply. People say how much she gives of herself in her groups. She writes personal letters to each woman in the groups and they report how the experience has impacted them in a tremendous way. She is also a great cook and likes to entertain people.

There are also many beautiful men who have influenced me over the years. Thomas Drew, the first male teacher I saw work with young children. His excellence in teaching 1st graders was remarkable. He retired this year and has over thirty years of teaching experience. He always supported me and he freely gave of himself to all of his students and his success rate is admirable.

Three male principals I worked for are also beautiful. Bobby Roper was the first principal I worked for at Lawndale Academy for four years.

Dr. Larry Thomas, who entrusted me to run an after-school tutoring program my first year teaching at his school. I was surprised and very encouraged because he had many other tenured teachers there and he chose me. He supported me without discriminating against me because of my age or years of teaching experience.

Calvin Watts was my last principal. He was a young man and he participated in many activities at Annistown

Elementary School. He was one of the first African American principals in a Gwinnett County public school. He always was available to listen to any concerns I had. He's a great role model and a trail blazer. I really respect him.

Phillip Todd is beautiful because he works with young children with disabilities and also works at a children's shelter.

Jeff Barksdale, my former supervisor is beautiful. He works with young people in sometimes challenging situations. He is a counselor and he tries to teach positive values to the people he works with.

James Dutton, a former co-worker and also provider of my post graduate degree supervision in counseling is a soft spoken wise man. His private practice advice has been very beneficial to me.

My father, Willie Douglas, is a beautiful man. Life hasn't always been easy for him and he made some poor choices early in his life, but he is an over comer. He has worked hard to raise eight children in the inner city of Chicago and he always provided us with food, clothing and shelter and some extras. We were always going on vacations and trips to the country. He exposed his children to a life outside of the ghetto. He taught his children to be kind to others and to help people in need. My father fights for equal rights for people and he is always giving to others. As a child, I disliked going to the VA hospital or the senior citizen home to see people we didn't know or weren't related to, but my parents were teaching us how to be compassionate and charitable to others. I recall one vacation where he picked up a hitchhiker. It was weird to pick up a man we didn't know, and on top of that, we already had a pretty full van and the man had to squeeze in. He appreciated the ride. Today I don't recommend picking up hitchhikers, but I have actually done it a time or two myself. It is ironic that the things I didn't like about my father as a child are some of the things I practice as an adult. Again, I don't recommend picking up strangers, but I did help some women who were in need of assistance. I respect my father's desire to give to people who don't have much, if any, support from others. Although I had a long time period of feeling angry and distant from my father, today we are close and have talked about my emotional issues from my childhood.

Parents, it is important that you show your children how special they are in words, as well as in actions. Tell them that they have gifts and talents that the world needs. Praise and encourage them from the time they can talk and respond to you. You did it when they were infants. You encouraged them to talk, walk, play and interact appropriately with others, so keep praising them as they grow and mature.

I have been critical in the past of adults being affectionate with their parents, but I do see the value in being visibly loved by your parents. Many people today are love starved. They desperately need a hug and a word of encouragement. It should start at home.

My four brothers are all beautiful in different ways. William (Bill) is a father of three children, an excellent trombone player, overall music lover and all around nice guy.

Stephen, my fire fighter brother, has always been a source of support for my family. He is generous, kind-hearted, fun to be around, and always willing to help his family in times of need.

Michael, my quiet brother, is a hard worker. He has made some tough choices early in his life, but he always comes back home to his upbringing. He is in a better place in his life now.

Jason, my youngest brother, is the entertainer of the family. He always has us laughing which lightens the mood and changes your attitude. He's a father, a husband, and he plays the piano for his church. He often has worked with the young people in his church.

Desmond Davis, my sister Sharon's husband, is a hard-working, quiet intelligent man. He's driven to be successful and is well on his way. He's a good husband to my sister and their children.

Milton Stennis is my favorite uncle. I call him my favorite because he calls all of his nieces his favorite niece. He's a loving, generous family man. He worked at the phone company for over thirty years. He is a positive role model to his sons as well as to other young men.

Donald Cook, my first serious boyfriend, was and will always be special to me. He told me how much he loved me when we dated as teenagers. He made me feel beautiful when I couldn't see it myself.

Mike Neal, my uncle, is a beautiful man because he not only survived the Cabrini Green projects of Chicago, but he is now an entrepreneur and successful businessman who mentors young men that have had some difficulty in their past gaining employment.

My grandfather, Albert White, I have gotten to know and love since I was 30 years old, is a special man. He is a wise, sweet and generous man who has helped me learn about my family roots. His knowledge is invaluable and I will treasure it always. He's my only living grandparent and he is very special to me.

I also have a relationship with Pamela Colbert and Charles White, my aunt and uncle. They are two of my grandfather's other children.

I was able to visit my aunt Pam, several years ago and I met her sister, Daphne, another aunt. She looks just like my mother and she has a son named Steve, also. It's ironic how people who are related but have never met, have so much in common because there is a special bond in the family.

To my precious, wonderful, beautiful husband, Kweku Davis, you have truly enhanced my life in many ways. You encourage and support my dreams and desires. You are an answer to my prayers. You are an excellent father to our son, Isaiah, and you tell me how beautiful I am to you. You truly make me feel beautiful when I am with you. I thank God for you daily and pray that our son will grow up imitating your gentle spirit, compassion, integrity, work ethics and dedication towards others.

Finally, to my darling son, Isaiah Emmanuel Davis, I prayed for you for many years before you were born. You are so special and beautiful. I had faith to believe I would be married and a mother before I turned 40 years old and it happened. My prayer is for you to become a great man that will be a blessing to others as you share your gifts with them.

Observations About Beauty

Nature is beautiful. I have observed many animals and watched their habits. They have had to adapt to the changes in their environment, largely due to man destroying their natural habitat. Birds never worry about what they are going to eat. They look for food and search until they find it. They fly together in flocks and support a tired or wounded bird. They are content with what they are. They don't try to conform to what someone else says. They are birds. I've never seen a bird trying to be a lion, fish, tiger, or a monkey. They naturally are birds and they behave like birds. It is people that try to change themselves into something other than what they were intended to be.

Many relationships have ended because people weren't really being themselves. They had no authenticity. They conformed to whoever they were in a relationship with at that time and it could only last for so long. Tragically some relationships end in death from abuse that could have possibly been avoided if only the person saw how beautiful and valuable they were. They wouldn't put themselves into a dangerous situation if they had self love. Loving yourself is so critical. You can't truly love others unless you know and love yourself. Anything else is only temporary, fake and even dangerous.

Beauty is like flowers. There are many types of flowers in the world and each one is beautiful and has a function. Some are pleasing to look at but they can deceive you. The venus fly trap is an example. If an insect gets close to that flower they get snapped up and they die. Some flowers have aromatic fragrances that people use on their bodies or in their homes. Some flowers are poisonous and some are edible. People are beautiful like flowers. We have a function in society. We are all beautiful in different ways because God made us beautiful.

Beauty has many layers like an onion. Beauty can be used to add to the people you encounter. Sometimes you have to dig deep into the layers of yourself to find your beauty but it is flavorful and tasty when you find it. It is like a buried treasure. You may have to dig for it for a long time but it is worth it when you uncover it. Beauty is like seasoning. It brings flavor to the lives of people.

Characteristics of Beauty

Sometimes our beauty is recognized by other people easier than what we see ourselves. Whenever people repeatedly tell you something positive about your character that is one of your attributes of beauty. It may be a gift of serving people, a good business mind, being encouraging to others, a good work ethic, a forgiving spirit, a gentle way, being kind hearted, an excellent speaker or motivator. It may be being creative, imaginative, industrious, being wise or even having street savvy. All of these are attributes of beauty. I will briefly discuss sixteen attributes or characteristics of beauty which I think are invaluable and are essential for people to have in some measure to be successful in life.

Peace

    Peace is a characteristic of beauty. Peace is being able to be calm and not anxious in any given situation. When you are at peace you are confident that your situation will work out for the best. Peace means having an inner contentment. Peace is the opposite of being at war or worrying. I often feel like I am emotionally at war when I worry and I'm not content about a problem. I try to say and do relaxing things to help me achieve or maintain peace. When you are at peace, you are able to take some time and ponder the dilemma you are facing. You don't react in fear, confusion, desperation, or anger. Peace is the calming mechanism that in many ways keeps a person sane. Peace is a trait that many people, including myself, struggle with in times of trouble. I repeat positive affirmations and call someone to talk about what is bothering me when I am troubled. Sometimes I lie down and take a nap, just to be at peace. Peace is being steady and not waivering in your faith when you are tested with the trials of life.

Roberta James, a friend of mind, exhibits this character. She is a graceful, gentle, woman of peace. Whenever she enters the room, I feel at peace and her presence and spirit is calming. As a mother of twin sons, one with cerebral palsy, she has experienced many trips to the hospital, surgeries, and close calls to death because of her son's health condition. She has had to miss numerous social functions to take care of her son, but I have never heard her complain. She takes her role as a mother to be the most important one in her life. Roberta has to dress, feed, provide medications to and bathe her son. She talks to him, plays music for him to enjoy and they play games together. They have a special way of communicating with each other. She has raised her sons alone with occasional help and assistance from other friends, family and health care providers. Roberta even had her own cleaning business for a while. I have personally watched Roberta with her sons and I am in awe of how she keeps herself and her family together. Roberta's sons are now 22 years old. Terry attends school and has a caregiver or respite worker assisting him, while Roberta is working and attending school to become a nurse. Larry is also working and wants to attend college in the near future. Roberta is a woman of peace and that makes her beautiful.

Having a Sense of Belonging

Having a sense of belonging is beautiful. I experienced this when I went to Africa. I was 25 years old and it was my first time flying. I flew for 16 hours from Chicago to Nigeria with a stop in London. I was scared when I went because at that time Nigeria was in a state of civil unrest. I had to stay at a hotel near the airport my first night because people were looting and burning up part of Lagos. After my initial fear of being killed in Africa in a war was over, I looked around and I'll never forget the feeling I felt when I stepped off of the plane. I saw people who looked like me everywhere. Their voices were melodic to my ears. They smiled at me and when they asked if I was American, and I said, "Yes," some said welcome home. I truly felt a sense of acceptance. It was almost overwhelming. I felt like I belonged. I felt like I was with my own people. I stood taller, I smiled at people and said hello to strangers, but they felt like my family. My two-week visit was incredible. I call it my honeymoon to Africa. I'll always be grateful to Presley Alohan for taking me to Africa and allowing me the opportunity to truly feel like I belonged somewhere.

Many African Americans don't know their family roots from Africa and I am one of them. It makes you feel like a piece of your life is missing and unanswered. I felt special in Nigeria. When you feel a sense of belonging, you truly do gain confidence. You walk with a purpose and a strong sense of pride. You become generous to others and you are not critical. I saw the poorest people in Nigeria as well as visited a king and queen of the Ado tribe in their mansion. All of the people had a strong sense of pride. Young boys worked daily to make money selling food, or rubber boots for flooded areas where tourists walked. I wore my boots and felt special as I waded through several city streets to a beach area. I enjoyed the foods, smells, and sounds of music and children playing. I was even okay visiting people without air conditioning and even electricity for several hours. The city didn't have enough electricity to go around. I truly learned how to be thankful for all of the things we take for granted in the US as an American citizen. The people were very kind to me and asked me many questions about America. They helped me identify with my roots and I truly was sad when I had to leave and come back to Chicago. It was a beautiful and unforgettable experience.

Many young people lack a sense of belonging today. They don't get it from home and they look for it elsewhere. They will search for it in the streets through gangs, drugs, alcohol, sex, violence, music or some other negative way. A significant amount of music has lyrics promoting violence and criminal behavior as a way of everyday life as a positive thing to do. I believe that much of it has to do with not knowing where you belong. If you know who you are and who you belong to, you can stand up to peer pressure easier. You won't use negative words and actions to fit in. Music is a powerful tool. It works on your emotions.

Many young people feel like they can relate to the lyrics of some music and that it is a way to express themselves in a manner they can't at home or at school.

Gang members have a strong allegiance. They will and do give their lives up for their gang members. They treat each other like a family, even if it is a very negative and dysfunctional one. This character trait of belonging is critical to everyone's self-esteem. It says I am here, I am special, and I am with you.

A sense of belonging is such a powerful character that people join cults and other organizations that they feel they can relate to. Numerous people have been seriously hurt or have died, because they were involved in a cult or some other type of organization that required their full devotion and noncompromising obedience. People who have left these groups often have undergone tremendous emotional stress and strain and have had to be deprogrammed and counseled for long periods of time because it is hard for them to leave that group of people or their way of thinking.

On a positive note, when you feel a sense of belonging, you can unite and overcome great obstacles, which leads me to my next characteristic of beauty.

Fulfilling Your Purpose

Knowing and fulfilling your purpose is definitely beautiful. Many people live their lives and never feel truly fulfilled. They go through their life day after day with an empty feeling. Work is not enough, family and friends are not enough. They feel a void, an open space. They are not fulfilled. Often times they seek ways, relationships, or vices to fill this void, but to no avail. They are still unfulfilled. They lack their purpose. When you know what your purpose is and you are actively following it, you are fulfilled. You wake up daily knowing what you are going to do. You get excited about what each day will bring, the people you will encounter and the experiences you will have. You are joyful and full of hope and expectation. You are confident that your needs will be met as you pursue your purpose.

There is a popular book out now about finding your purpose and I read it, and it has truly changed my life as well as confirmed some things I have believed but have been insecure to act on. I highly recommend reading "The Purpose Driven Life" by Rick Warren. This book put me in touch with my purpose. Writing this book is one of the manifestations of my purpose.

Oprah Winfrey is a great example of a woman fulfilling her purpose. She has touched the lives of millions of people and she will continue to do so. She is generous and compassionate. Her life means a lot to many people. She didn't allow her humble beginnings to stop her from achieving greatness. She is well known around the world. She is a purpose driven woman and that makes her beautiful.

My favorite book, "I Know Why the Caged Bird Sings" by Maya Angelou, is another example of fulfilling your purpose. Maya suffered through rape and abandonment and stopped talking for a time period. She overcame her trauma and is now a world renowned author, educator, poet, director, producer, civil rights activist and historian. She has written many books and speeches and even delivered a poem for the inauguration of a US president. She has inspirational cards and her words truly encourage my heart. Like the caged bird that sings because it knows its purpose, Maya Angelou is fulfilling her purpose and that makes her beautiful.

A final example of being purpose driven is during the civil rights movement. Many Americans came together to fight for justice and equality in America. The fight still continues but because of the civil rights movement, minorities of all kinds can have freedom and privileges that the US had once restricted them from. We can vote, eat wherever we want, work in any career, sit wherever we want, sleep at any hotel and live in any community because of the civil rights movement. Things are not truly equal today, but the balance has been shifted and more rights are being enjoyed today because of the blood, sweat, tears, beatings, lynching, incarcerations and ultimately deaths of many fearless people who had a sense of purpose and were united in that purpose.

When people unite together, things will happen. Each of us must find our purpose and actively pursue it and we can and will change our society for the better. There is true beauty in fulfilling your purpose.

Wisdom is Beautiful

The bible records King Solomon as the wisest man alive. He was given wisdom because he asked for it. There is a scripture in the Bible in the book of James that says if anyone asks God for wisdom he will give it to him. Why is wisdom important to have? We go through life daily making choices. We have to interact with other people and at times this will be challenging. We don't always agree with one another, but we have to live with each other.

Wisdom is the ability to discern what the right action in a situation is. Wisdom is being able to solve problems and make choices for ourselves and sometimes others, in the most advantageous way. A wise man makes the choice that is beneficial for everyone involved whenever possible. Wisdom doesn't mean that everyone will be happy but that the solution is the one option that will benefit people the most. When you are wise, everyone won't agree with your decision or be on your side, but you must stand by your decision.

A child will ask his parent for unhealthy things to eat and when told they can't have it, they won't be happy, but it is for their health and in their best interest not to have it. Parents need wisdom to raise their children. Seek advice when you are unsure of what to do from a person who has a track record of being wise. It will help you a great deal.

A wise person is often a peacemaker. They mediate for people. They listen to both sides involved in a situation and offer an impartial, informed choice.

Wisdom is critical for all people to have in some measure. It could have stopped me from making some poor choices in my past like I mentioned previously. If I had been wise as a teenager, I wouldn't have put myself in some life threatening situations. I have prayed for wisdom over the years and I believe I have a measure that is beneficial to me today.

Dr. Shelton, a psychiatrist at GRN is a wise woman. She works with children and adolescents in a mental health facility. She has to decide if and which medications to prescribe to her patients. She has to educate the parents and her patients about the medications, side effects and deal with compliance issues. She is gentle but firm in her decisions. Her goal is to improve the quality of life for her patients and it isn't always convenient or pleasant to work with a child with a disability, but it is required that she does what she feels is best. Wisdom allows her to make these choices. I admire and respect her. She is a woman of beauty because she utilizes wisdom in her practices. She also mentors others in her profession and assists them with their careers.

Parents, you all have been given a gift of wisdom. Utilize it. You know more than your children do and it is your job to raise them by applying wisdom. Listen to your inner voice. If you are unsure about something, seek advice. Don't allow your children to manipulate you into giving them things that are unhealthy for them. If you are a couple, work together. Don't let the children use you against each other. If one parent says, "No," then the answer is no. Discuss in private any differences you have. Don't argue in front of your children. Provide a united front. Differences can be worked on when your children aren't around. Have family time to discuss issues with your children. Let them know that their input is considered, but never agree to things that aren't beneficial for them. Listen to your child and learn what your child's temperament and overall character are. Be an advocate for your children, but don't cover up wrong doings or choices your children make. There are some consequences that are natural and some that are enforced. Teach your children to use wisdom. They see what you do and they learn from it. They learn negative and positive things so be wise. Let your no mean no and your yes mean yes. That's using wisdom!

Love is Beautiful

There are many types of love. Love for one another, also called brotherly love. Many people need to work on this type of love. Love for an inanimate object like food, games, clothes, and other material things. There is a love for our creator, a power greater than us. Love is a feeling or emotion that we share with others. Many people don't know the true meaning of love. They confuse it with lust, or with control. Love is freedom with responsibility. When you love someone, you want the best for them. You enjoy seeing them happy and you stand beside them when they need support. A true test of love is during times when a person is not showing love to you. There is an expression that the people closest to you hurt you the most. This is true because you have allowed them to get into your heart and the heart is vulnerable to hurt and pain. Love also is a great emotion as well as an action.

When you love someone, you tell them in words and deed. I remember receiving a cake from my boyfriend, Donald Cook, when I was around 16 years old. It was an "I love you cake." It wasn't my birthday or any other special day. It was a "just because" cake. I'll never forget how much I felt loved and to this day I am still close with his parents even though our dating relationship didn't last. Donald showed me that I was worthy to be loved at a time when I felt unlovable.

Showing love means also making tough decisions. Using wisdom with love is critical to avoid making costly mistakes. The words we say can cut worse than a knife and hurtful words are not loving. People have strained relationships or don't speak to each other because of unloving words as well as actions. Positive words are healing and helping words. They lift you up when you feel down and love can bring a smile to your face.

When you love someone, you are able to overlook their shortcomings. No one is perfect and we make mistakes, but if you show love, you will forgive people. Love does not mean accepting any type of abuse or mistreatment. You have to love yourself first before you can love someone else. It does mean talking about the situation and letting that person know how they offended you. Maybe you can't talk to the person or choose not to because is it too painful. Write a letter to them and express your feelings. You may never mail it but writing it can be a part of forgiving and releasing them. I'll talk more about forgiveness later.

Maybe you can't say you love yourself right now. It may because of some past hurts or choices you have made.

Remember, you are a lovable person no matter what was done to you by someone else or by your own choices. Love covers a multitude of situations. People never go to their graves thinking about the material things they can't take with them. Many people have severed relationships with family members over trivial things. Remember that life is truly short. Tomorrow isn't promised. Love that person and move forward.

Lorraine Puerta is a woman who loves deeply. I called her the mother of GRN when I worked there. She talked to everyone and made them feel as happy as possible during their visits. Lorraine has defused many situations with her voice and her demeanor. She survived the death of her husband several years ago. Last year when her dog died, Lorraine was surprised when many of the GRN staff, past and present, chipped in and bought her a puppy. Lorraine loves Max and we felt that she would benefit from having another dog at home. You never know the impact your love has on others. When Lorraine was not at GRN, people asked about her and commented that the atmosphere was different in her absence.

Love does impact humans at the greatest level. The heart! Many of the hurts or unjust policies and actions of the world exist because of a lack of love and compassion for others. If we all loved each other more, we would be more tolerant of others and overall be happier.

Parents, tell your children you love them. Hug them and tell them how special they are to you. Learn to love yourself if you don't. Look at yourself and find value in yourself. You are a lovable and capable person. Love is a oneness that can't be replaced with anything else.

Love is beautiful.

Humor is Beautiful

Having a good sense of humor is beautiful. Have you ever been in a bad mood and a person walks in and smiles at you and you automatically feel better? I've been told that I have a good sense of humor. By no way do I consider myself to be a comedian, but I do tend to have people smiling and laughing when we talk. Humor is the ability to make people smile, laugh and lighten the mood and enjoy the lighter side of life. We need humor to survive. A wise person is able to laugh and say, "Hey, life's not perfect and neither am I, but I will survive."

Humor puts pep in your step. When you feel humorous, you can relate to others in a positive manner. It encourages everyone involved. A good joke can lighten a mood. A person with a good sense of humor makes people feel good and when you feel good you do good things and that is beautiful.

There are several comedians that I respect and admire. I tend to prefer the ones who tell clean jokes, but I do like some of the others. I enjoy Bill Cosby and Sinbad. I have several movies from the '70's that Bill Cosby was in with Sidney Poitier. They were hilarious. I also enjoyed the Cosby show in the 1980's. I would rush home to see the show and I still watch the reruns now. Cosby dealt with real life situations in a humorous way.

My father is also a humorous man. I guess that is where I get my sense of humor. My father has a nickname for just about everyone he meets. When I had my son, I couldn't wait to hear what nickname my dad would have for him. The nicknames he chooses don't have anything to do with the person, they are just a name my dad picks. My husband's name is Kweku(Quay coo) and some people find it difficult to pronounce. Many people call him Q. My father calls him Q and calls our son barbeque. We think it's funny. His grandkids call him Kadoodle! They made it up and it has stuck with him.

Humor can be a type of affection. As I mentioned, many people have nicknames. To this day, I don't know the real names of some people I grew up with. I have to really think hard. We had some cute and weird nicknames; Boo, Curly, Dump, man, shorty, Blackie, and pump belly, to name a few. I'm smiling while writing this section and thinking about some of the names we called people.

One note of caution, humor is only humorous when the person is not offended. Calling me bald- headed as a child was never funny to me. It actually hurt me deeply and contributed to my low self-esteem. Teasing a person with a disability is also not humorous. It can truly hurt a person for a lifetime. Another note to consider, people grow up and often times they don't want to still be called their childhood nickname and definitely not in front of other people. Be considerate with your humor.

Millions, if not billions, of dollars are made from humor. Look at the number of talk show and late night talk shows and don't forget talk radio, internet, and satellite TV. They can find something people will think is funny in just about any situation. I again caution you to not use humor to hurt people. I don't agree with things that can destroy another person's self-esteem or image in the name of fun.

Think of the last time you laughed at yourself. Has it been a while or can you even remember it? If not, lighten up! Enjoy life, laugh and smile. Humor is beautiful.

Serving Others is Beautiful

When you need help with something, who comes to your mind? Does a particular friend or family member's name immediately come to your mind? Who is always serving others in some capacity? Is it you? Do people compliment you on your dedication to helping others, your volunteer work, church group, social club, charity, team or group activities? If so, you have the gift of service. Do you naturally show hospitality to people? Are you volunteering your time, talent, treasure and yourself on a regular basis? Do you value making the lives of others more fruitful? A person who serves others gains joy when they are able to be a server and a blessing to others. When you serve, you receive so much personally. We are often so busy with our own lives that we sometimes forget that it is more blessed to give than to receive.

We all need to assist others. No matter what our situation is we can help serve someone else periodically. Short on money, volunteer your time. An encouraging phone call or visit can help cheer someone up. Cooking a meal or cleaning up a room in a home is serving. Answering phone calls at a call center or a hotline is serving. Pledging money to an organization is serving. Setting up and taking down chairs for a function is serving. Driving someone to run errands is serving. As you are reading this section, think about the last time you served someone and how you felt. I know I feel a certain sense of joy when I help others. Think of the last time you were served. How did it make you feel? We truly feel good when we help someone else. You never know that your service could help a person who was feeling helpless and discouraged. At the least, it should put a smile on their face and yours temporarily.

Kathy Lewis is a true servant. She is a beautiful person. I know that I can count on her whenever I need her. She has sent me cards and has cooked meals for me and my family on several occasions. It truly encouraged my heart. She has provided transportation to people to church, the grocery store and other places. She picked up my mother from the airport when I was in labor with my son. She didn't hesitate to do it and she didn't ask for anything in return. She picked my mother up one day to give her a break from the house, took her shopping and for a visit at her house. My mom was so appreciative and so was I. I know that Kathy is blessed by serving others and her needs are met. I truly appreciate her heart.

By nature, being a servant has a negative connotation. It has meant being beneath someone and catering to their every whim. African Americans were often placed in servant positions and weren't paid well. Slavery was an even greater disservice to African Americans. They served people without pay and respect. Today, we don't have legal slavery in America, but people are still treated in a subservient manner.

Minorities are often discounted or disrespected and given menial jobs. Those jobs need to be performed just as much as the non menial jobs.

If we didn't have garbage workers, how would our health be in our communities? If we didn't have waiters and maids, how would our hospitality and food industries suffer? Serving is important.

Poverty is all around us and people are often treated in a negative manner if they are poor. This shouldn't be. Many times, and I have been guilty of this myself, I have looked at a homeless person or a person on the street and thought to myself that they should get a job. I don't know that person's situation. Many people are only a paycheck away from being homeless themselves. I know how I have struggled financially in the last couple of years myself.

I remember when I was a school teacher. The janitorial staff and lunchroom staff were often overlooked and not considered professionals like the teachers. I found this distasteful. I always tried to treat everyone with the same amount of respect. We all had a job to do. If the school was unclean or unsafe, we couldn't work there. If the food wasn't prepared, we couldn't eat there. All jobs are necessary and are worthy of respect.

A servant is actually the greatest person. They get to see what is truly going on in a person's life and not some façade we present to others on the outside. A person who serves is truly a beautiful person. Serve someone today and you'll reap the benefits yourself.

Perseverance is Beautiful

Perseverance is a character of beauty. Life circumstances can challenge the core of a person's existence. Death, poverty, injustice, financial difficulties, relationship problems, work issues and health challenges are just some obstacles that we will encounter as we go through life. Not everyone has all of theses issues, but we all have at least one of them. No one is immune from trouble. Money, power and prestige do not have immunity from struggles and/or hardships. Often when we have an issue to overcome, it has a domino effect and triggers other problems. How do we survive? By persevering.

Perseverance is the ability to overcome and endure the hardships of life. It is by no means easy, but it is definitely needed for your survival. Some people suffer from depression when they encounter a challenge. Some fight for a while and when they feel pressured they seek support from others. They persevere until the challenge is over. A challenge is like a storm. It can wreak havoc on your property and even a loss of life may occur, but it does pass. When it's over, the people who have survived pick up the pieces of their lives again by rebuilding or repairing the damage that has occurred. They start again. They build a house that is stronger than the one they lost. They build a house made to endure storms. They give thanks for being alive and able to start again. They acknowledge the power that the storm has, but they understand that they are survivors, and this strengthens their character. It is beautiful to see people work together through tribulation.

Hurricane Katrina is an example of perseverance. Hundreds of thousands of people were displaced and lost everything they owned, including some loved ones, but many are rebuilding their lives. Some have government assistance, but many don't. I heard a story about an 80 year old man in New Orleans that was rebuilding his house with his own hands a little bit at a time. He doesn't complain about what happened or the lack of support he is receiving. He just perseveres and keeps on rebuilding his house. That is the beauty of perseverance.

Patience is Beautiful

Patience is a virtue is a common expression. It is required when a person desires something and it doesn't happen immediately. Patience is a sister to perseverance. Patience is calmly waiting. I'll repeat that. Patience is calmly waiting. It is not being anxious, worried, nervous, upset or stressed while you wait to receive what you desire. It's ironic how a person of faith may still struggle with patience. I know I am working on this character trait, even though I have seen many blessings and/or miracles in my own life.

What is difficult for me seems to be enduring the storm. I know it's going to end, but it's challenging to go through a difficult situation not knowing how long it will last. It is similar to pregnancy and childbirth. When I was pregnant, I knew that in nine months a baby would be born, but it seemed to take an eternity for the time to come. In my case, my labor was induced and ultimately I had to have an emergency cesarean section. I was uncomfortable at first and then I was in pain. I knew I would love my baby, but I had to endure some pain until he arrived. It was definitely worth it. My son is a beautiful healthy child.

When I am not patient, it affects my body and nerves in a negative way. I sweat; bite my nails, and I pace the floor. My heart rate increases and I am overall unhappy. I know that many people can relate to this. I have even had some sleepless nights and have cried on the floor a time or two.

What is ironic is that doing these things doesn't change my situation one bit. Time is not going to go any faster by my impatience. In fact, it seems to go slower. It's like a child waiting to be disciplined by their parent. They want it to be over; so they ask them when they are going to punish them. They get upset when they have to wait to be punished. They keep looking at their parent wondering if they have forgotten or if they are thinking up the worst possible punishment. Usually, the stress of not being patient is worse than the actual punishment.

In a society of microwaves, fast food restaurants, drive-thru windows, fast cars, cell phones and other electronic gadgets that we say make life easier, it's a challenge for many people to wait. Road rage is more common today, especially in a traffic jam. Violence is more prevalent, occurring at sporting events, concerts and other performances, from spectators as well as the entertainers and athletes. People get run over and even trampled to death occasionally in large gatherings when people are not patient. It is a sad and unnecessary thing.

Panic, anxiety, fear and rage are all opposites of patience. People who lose their will to fight often have lost patience as well as hope. You can't succeed in life without going through challenges and being patient will help you have an easier time. When you are patient, you are happier and healthier. Many people who aren't patient suffer from illness, diseases and stress. These affect all areas of their lives. Stress can and does cause physical issues and illness in many people. There are many advertisements for books, pills, tapes, relaxation techniques, therapy and other remedies to alleviate stress and anxiety in your life. Stress can contribute to mental illness. I have personally seen this working as a mental health practitioner. Some of my clients can't leave the house, go to school or go out into the community because of stress and fear. They are not equipped to deal with life issues in a positive way. I have to work with them to learn how to be patient and relax before they can work on their other issues.

Lack of patience can impair your ability to make sound decisions. You become impatient, impulsive and react in negative ways. Impatience can cause misunderstandings. You listen better when you are patient. You can hear what the other person is saying and even if you don't agree with them, being patient allows you opportunities to communicate with them and possibly come to a compromise. Patience it being confident that you will see the end result of whatever situation you are in, whether the outcome be positive or negative. A patient person is at peace. They recognize that they can't rush time and that things happen that are out of their control. They realize that they can control their actions and emotions, which is better than being frustrated, impatient and possibly losing relationships.

Sounds difficult? It really isn't. As I am writing this, I am telling myself to practice what I preach. I must become a master of patience, because trials are a certainty. Patience will help you overcome the trials.

Patience is a rule of society. It's built into sports and laws. A whistle is blown if a player makes a false move in football and track. A basketball player is given a foul for pushing another player to get the ball. You get penalized in many sports for not exercising patience.

There are laws that limit how fast you can drive and traffic signals and signs that tell you when you can go or have to stop. There are limitations on what age a person can drive, drink or legally be an adult.

Being patient produces maturity. A child cries because he wants something. He doesn't know that his bottle has to be prepared or that his food may be too hot to eat right away. As he matures and gets older, he learns to be patient. He doesn't know that he needs teeth to eat what the grown ups are eating, but in time he is eating solid food. Parents must teach their children to be patient so they can interact with other people appropriately. Patience means not now, but in due time and being patient is truly a beautiful thing.

Faith is Beautiful

Faith is a characteristic of beauty. Faith believes that what you want will happen without seeing the proof. It is the ability to predict your dreams and goals and seeing them materialize in the future. When you have faith, you don't have doubts about the ending outcome of a situation. I have had great examples of faith in my life as well as in others.

In 1993, I decided to pursue a career in teaching. Renee Muhammad told me about a program that offered free tuition to people who had bachelors' degrees in fields other than teaching. My degree was in psychology. I inquired about the program and was determined to get into it. The demand was high because it was a competitive program and several hundred people applied for it. The program required a four year commitment to teaching in a Chicago public school.

I should have never even applied, according to the requirements. I had a grade point average of 3.01 and the requirement was 3.50. I still applied. I knew that I wanted to be a teacher and I wanted to get into the special program. I didn't even tell anyone about the requirement. I was confident that I would be accepted. I passed the first three steps of the program's application without incident. I should have been eliminated because of my GPA, but I wasn't. I interviewed with the school staff and I was confident that I was one of the hundred people accepted for the program.

When the letter came in the mail denying me a position for the program, I was devastated. I didn't understand what had happened. I had done everything right. I believed and I applied. I was supposed to be in that program. I stormed the floor of my apartment crying. I had stepped out in faith and I didn't receive what I wanted.

A month later I received a phone call from the Chicago public school system. Someone had declined the offer and they were offering the spot to me. I was ecstatic! I got into the program.

I have come to learn that having faith requires patience as well as perseverance. An obstacle will always present itself before you receive your blessing. I have never just walked into a true desire without my faith being challenged. If I knew for sure what would happen, it wouldn't allow me the opportunity to be a woman of faith.

Another example of faithful people is Bishop Gary Hawkins Sr. and first lady, Elder Debbie Hawkins. They are the leaders of Voices of Faith Ministries, the church I attend. In less than fifteen years, they have built a ministry that began in their home to 30 people, including children, meeting at a recreational center. Today, they have two churches in two counties, a daycare center, acquired an academy and a membership of over 11,000. They truly practice what they preach about faith. It is beautiful, but it wasn't always easy for them. They also had obstacles to overcome and they did so by utilizing their faith.

Your faith will always be tested. I have increased my faith over the years. Each situation has made me a stronger person. Faith comes in different levels. Some people only have a small amount of faith and others have a larger amount. The larger your faith is, the greater the victory. What do you want? Ask for it, believe that you have received it and don't waiver. It may not come today or when you want it, but when you exercise your faith you receive far more than what you asked for.

One final note about faith: Faith is a personal characteristic with a lot of responsibility. You have to use it wisely. You can't ask for things that will hurt other people or are just simply for your pleasure. You can enjoy the fruits of faith personally, but a truly faithful person wants to help others and they believe that what they are asking for will assist them in helping people. Sometimes you have to be faithful for others when they can't. I know that life does bring about pain and hurt. I am by no means, saying that anything you believe in you will receive if it is negative or not planned for your life. Trials will come and having faith doesn't eliminate them. Faith is a key to open the door to being fulfilled and joyful and to having favor in your life. I believe that God rewards people who are faithful, but again faith isn't some magic potion. Faith is a gift. Use it wisely and it will show you its beauty!

Hope is Beautiful

Hope is a key element to faith. Hope is what puts faith in action. Hope is waiting for what you want to come true. It is an expectation. While faith is being confident in what you believe without seeing the proof, hope is the boat that keeps faith afloat. Jesse Jackson has a phrase, "Keep hope alive." This expression has been embedded in my mind. Whenever things don't go the way I would like them to, I often say, "I must keep hope alive. Things will change. My situation will improve and this too shall pass." These are just a few of the phrases I say to keep my spirit up in times of trial, tribulation and/or trouble. Where there is hope there is life; because you will persevere, you will have faith. You will not only survive but be an overcomer.

Hope is a character trait that has literally saved lives. Have you heard news stories of people who have survived storms, earthquakes and other tragedies and have lived to tell about it? Some people kept themselves alive because they had the hope that they would see their loved ones again. Rescue workers hope to find survivors in rubble, debris and other elements. They are often amazed at the people who survive, sometimes days, in the worst situations. These people are often injured, but they never gave up hope. They did whatever they had to to stay alive.

Runaway slaves utilized hope. They didn't know what the outcome of running away would be, but they believed that they would find freedom. They couldn't read or ask people for assistance. They hoped that the path they were on would take them to freedom. They didn't worry about what they would eat or how long the journey would take. They had hope of a better life for themselves and possibly their family.

If it weren't for hope, many of us wouldn't be in the position we are in today. As mentioned earlier, the civil rights movement was critical to the success and opportunities that we have in America today. People were unified, full of faith, hope, ambition and they were purpose driven. This combination is part of the winning ticket to being successful in life.

Hope keeps you determined to accomplish the things you want to materialize in your life.

Several people come to my mind when I think of examples of hope. My sister, Mariann Douglas, is one of them. She is attending school to become a nurse. She has struggled for years as a single mother of two children. She has gone from full time to part time to time off from school over the past several years. She has worked at two different part time jobs while she has been in school. She has always kept her hope of becoming a nurse alive. She has never given up. I am confident that she will achieve her goal because she is hopeful.

My two cousins, K'hari and Y'kheyo Underwood, are also examples of young men that utilize hope frequently. They have a real estate business together. They work together to make a success of themselves despite the challenges they face as young landlords and businessmen. I have seen K'hari work on several business ventures that didn't work out the way he had expected, but he didn't give up. He believed in his dream to be successful and he is well on his way. He is always trying to improve himself and he shares information with others. Y'kheyo has always supported his brother.

A key element to hope is having positive people as examples in your life. Who do you look up to and respect? Who can teach you and assist you with your goals? Who has already done what you would like as a map for you to follow? Are there people on a consistent basis encouraging you? These thing will give you hope.

A final thing you need to utilize hope is positive affirmations. These could be scriptures from the Bible or some other book. They could be expressions you have heard or read. Many people read daily thoughts to meditate on for the day. This is also a way to encourage yourself. I try to keep thoughts or messages on my voice mail at home. I have had people call for business or even a wrong number leave me a message saying that they appreciated the thought I had on my voice mail.

Monica Douglas Davis

I try to encourage people to stay positive, utilize faith and have hope.

Having hope is truly beautiful!

Encouragement is Beautiful

Being encouraging to others is a characteristic of beauty. Encouragement is the ability to share a positive word or deed with someone when they need it. It may be saying, "You can do it. I believe in you. It will all work out. Way to go." It may be visiting someone sick or incarcerated. Encouragement is a component of serving. When you encourage someone, you give of yourself to help build them up. Encouragement can assist in building another person's confidence. It helps them feel successful that they can achieve their goal or overcome an obstacle they are facing.

I remember watching cheerleaders at sporting events. They hype up not only the players of their team, but the audience. They shout and yell to encourage their team to win.

Team members also encourage one another. They pat each other, high five and say positive words to their teammates. A team that was losing has come back to win and be victorious because they were encouraged that they could win. They felt confident and they played better.

If we encouraged one another daily, I truly believe the world would be a happier, better place. We especially need to encourage our young people. Many young people that don't receive encouragement make some wrong choices that could endanger their lives. They get involved in gangs, prostitution, hanging with the wrong people, dropping out of school, unhealthy relationships, committing crimes, taking drugs and/or using alcohol. Some run away from home and live on the streets doing whatever they can to survive. I have rarely seen a young person who was encouraged to do well involved in these types of activities. Many teenage mothers were not encouraged at home. They looked for attention outside of their homes.

Sometimes you must encourage yourself. As I mentioned earlier, saying positive affirmations are beneficial. Words are powerful. Positive words can go a long way. I recall an exercise I saw years ago about the power of words. The speaker picked an audience member to assist him. He told them to hold out their strongest arm and not allow him to push it down. The speaker said negative words to the audience member on stage and teased him about being weak. When he pushed his arm, it quickly went down. Next the speaker told the person to think of positive things. He encouraged him to think that he was strong and happy and capable of keeping his arm up. When the speaker pushed on his arm this time, it didn't go down. It didn't go down even when he pushed with both hands. What was different? The person felt encouraged and strong the second time. The mind will manifest physically what we think. Think positive and you will receive positive results. Think negative and you'll have negative results. There is a proverb about the tongue being positive or negative. Encouragement is using your words to empower someone. It is powerful.

When you are feeling down and low, pick up the phone and call someone and say something positive to them. After your conversation you'll feel better in the midst of your situation. It is not uncommon to encourage someone and find that you receive assistance from them. Their mind is clear and they may also be able to help you think of options that you hadn't prior to talking to them. Communicating with someone in a positive manner allows the brain to be stimulated in a way that can be beneficial to you.

I have had many opportunities presented to me when I was encouraging someone else. I felt good helping the person. My attitude was positive and I attracted positive people to me. People have shared information or have provided me with resources that I was unaware of during times I have encouraged someone else. They may say, "I know someone who can help you, or has done what you want, or has experienced what you're going through and may be able to help you." At the very least, when you encourage someone else you don't have time to pity yourself and your situation.

When you encourage someone, it can enhance their life. Many depressed people don't receive consistent encouragement from anyone. They are unable to encourage themselves and they lose hope. When you lose hope, you become desperate and disillusioned. I definitely do see a place for therapy and/or medication to deal with depression, but encouragement is also critical to provide hope. If you don't feel hope, you won't take your medication or go to therapy. Encouragement will help a person take steps forward to recovery from any situation. It empowers them to fight and not give up in tough times. It is beautiful!

Gratitude is Beautiful

Gratitude is a trait of beauty. In a world full of war, hate, prejudice, injustice, greed, financial challenges, sickness and poverty, it can be difficult to focus on the positive things in life. As you are reading this book, you can be grateful that you can see, you can turn the pages of a book and you can read. These things are reasons to be grateful because not everyone can say the same thing. Being grateful is acknowledging the things we do have and can do, and not focusing on what we don't have or can't do. I know people that keep a daily journal of what they are grateful for.

Being grateful helps to keep you humble as well as put things in perspective. It gives you the opportunity to give thanks for all the things we take for granted. Life, health, our five senses, family, friends, other relationships, employment, and other things can be things we are grateful for. If you find that you can't think of anything to be grateful for, think of simple things you have, like clean running water, a place to live, food to eat and the function of your limbs. Many people outside of America don't have these things on a daily basis. America has its problems as well, but we can all think of people who have less. Watch the news and if no one we know is on the TV, we should be thankful. Tragedies occur daily and yes, we all have pain and trouble, but being grateful means we can realize that we can go on.

An example of being grateful is my mother, Mildred Douglas. She is always giving credit to God for all of the blessings she receives as well as blessings other people receive. This year my family surprised her for her birthday and traveled to Toledo, Ohio. When we rang the doorbell, she was very happy. My family has had some financial challenges this year and most of us were unable to buy her a gift, other than traveling to OH and paying for our lodging, food and gas. My mother didn't complain at all. She was able to fellowship with all of her family. Everyone was there, all eight children and their families, as well as my mother's sister and brother. That's challenging with such a big family. We had a great time! My mother has never been a hard woman to please. When I talked to my sisters and my aunt, we couldn't think of a gift to give her because she doesn't require much. My mother just wants her family to do well and she is grateful that we are. She doesn't want jewelry, fancy clothes, money, expensive meals or even fancy vacations. She is grateful to be alive to see her family as often as she can. When I think about my mother, she reminds me that material things are insignificant when you think about being alive another day. She is truly a grateful woman.

Can I guarantee you wealth, happiness and success daily? Absolutely not, but part of what happens to you is a mind set. If you are alive, you have things to be grateful for, as well as a chance to have a better attitude this day. Take the time right now to give thanks for at least five things. You don't have to limit yourself to only five. Take all the time you need. Be grateful and you are exhibiting a character of beauty.

Integrity is Beautiful

Integrity is a character trait of beauty. Integrity is being honest and just in any situation. It is standing up for what is right no matter who opposes you. This may be difficult in today's society. In a world where bribery is an everyday occurrence and the highest bid on information can bring wealth, integrity is not always evident. There's an expression that one hand washes the other hand. This isn't good when you are washing in dirty water. People are afraid that if they speak up for what is right, they will suffer in some way. Politics seem to be saying what you think people want to hear to get you into office, and not following what you said you would do. How often do you turn on the TV and hear about crimes that shock you? People have become desperate and they commit crimes that make me shudder.

One of the worst things about a crime is when there are people witnessing it, and they don't try to intervene in any way. When I was in my early twenties, I was attacked on a subway platform. I yelled for help, but no one watching, male or female, assisted me. I had to literally fight the man off of me. He was a mentally unstable man. I was lucky that he didn't hurt me, because I later learned that he had a record for assault and rape. My situation could have been avoided if one person had simply told the man to leave me alone.

There's a song out now about not snitching on someone when you see a crime being committed. I can't believe how this message can be taken seriously. Lives are at risk if we don't help each other. I definitely say that you have to proceed with caution. I'm not asking people to become police officers but to help one another when we see someone in possible danger. A cell phone call from a person observing a crime might save a life.

When you have integrity you realize that you won't always be popular. My favorite TV show is "Good Times". One episode was about the father finding $27,000 cash in a grocery store from a robbery. He turned the money in and was rewarded with a plaque and a $50 gift certificate from the store. The family received prank calls and even a dummy doll was delivered to their door for being a "dummy that turned in that money." James, the father, was upset and he revealed that he had actually found $29,000 and had kept $2,000. His family had to help him remember that he was a man of integrity and he agreed to give that money back as well. It was a struggle because the family lived in the Chicago housing projects and they could have really used that money, but when you are a person of integrity you ultimately do the right thing.

A person who displays integrity will be successful because he stands up for what is right and just. You may have to stand alone and not be a people pleaser, but you will sleep well each night knowing that you haven't betrayed your values or been manipulative to get what you want.

Integrity begins at home. How many times have you told your child to say or do something that isn't true? Maybe you told them to say you're not home when a person is on the phone that you don't want to talk to. Maybe you cheat on your taxes. Have you left the grocery store with extra items and you didn't return them? Some people call this a blessing but it is really stealing. You didn't pay for the groceries and they belong to someone else.

Being a person of integrity doesn't mean being perfect. You will make mistakes and actually we all will make some bad decisions. Integrity is consistently doing what is right, but no one has a 100% record of utilizing integrity. We all have some skeletons in our closet. I find it ironic that people who criticize others the most have some of the biggest transgressions themselves. It is even more amazing that people will criticize someone for the same thing they had done themselves but it hasn't been revealed yet. Integrity seems to be in short supply, but I still believe that there are people of integrity in our society who make the world a better place. Be a person of integrity, because integrity is beautiful!

Forgiveness is Beautiful

It can be difficult to forgive someone who you feel has done a wrong action to you. Forgiving someone means that you don't hold the offense against the person or people who harmed you in some way. This trait is one of the most difficult ones for most people to apply to their lives. If someone hurt you in your childhood, it can be a true challenge to forgive them. It may have been a parent, relative, close family friend, co-worker, teacher, coach, mentor, pastor, or someone else you trusted. Maybe a stranger hurt you. Maybe they were negligent in some manner or they abused you physically, emotionally, or mentally. You were an innocent child. The adults who should have nurtured and protected you were the ones who hurt you. It is a sad thing, but a reality far too often, that children are abused by someone they know and trust.

I have written a children's book about child sexual abuse that I will be publishing in the near future. It's a secret that unfortunately too many people have experienced. Abuse is no respecter of person. It covers all races, economic status, country, religion and culture. Many people who are incarcerated were abused and/or neglected early on in their lives. This in no way means that they are excused from the crimes they were convicted of committing. There are consequences for any action we take. I do believe that some of these people may have made some of the negative choices because of their past, because they don't know how beautiful they are. True beauty has to be learned for most of us. If you really love yourself, then you are capable of loving others and you can learn to be a forgiving person.

We all do know how to forgive people. We do it everyday. If someone does something we dislike that we don't consider a big deal, we let it go. If you are mistreated by someone in authority, you will usually show some self-control before you speak to them. You may just let the situation go. We all have family members, friends or co-workers that can be difficult to get along with. We may say, "That's just the way they are." We excuse their flaws. Why do we do this? We forgive them because we have some kind of investment in our relationship with them. It may be to keep peace at home, work or wherever we see them. We may dread seeing them and try to avoid them whenever we can, but we do tolerate them and overlook or forgive them more than we care to admit.

Forgiveness is so critical because it affects our lives on a daily basis. Forgiving someone is freeing. If you are harboring a grudge or have negative feelings about someone, I want you to stop and think about that person and that situation right now. Do you feel anger, uncomfortable or are you upset? Has your attitude and countenance changed from positive to negative? If so, you haven't forgiven them and they still have some control over your life. When you forgive someone, you release yourself from continual pain and stress. Thinking about past hurts only brings unhappiness to you. Let it go. Free your mind so you can truly enjoy your life. When you harbor unforgiveness, you can't fully enjoy life. You are cold, untrusting and, sometimes, unloving to other people. You have a dark secret that you know is affecting your relationships with others. Maybe you are in a relationship, but you can't be totally open and trusting of that person. You have built walls around yourself to protect yourself from being hurt. The past can effect the present and your future. Many people have lost opportunities to be loved because they haven't forgiven someone.

Unforgiveness eats at the core of your being. It affects your heart and your soul. It pollutes your mind so you can't see clearly. It prevents your mind from focusing on the positive things in life.

We all make choices that sometimes are not good. We all need forgiveness at some time sooner or later. Many of us need it daily. It could be an unkind word, look or gesture we made at someone. It could be being insensitive or unloving towards someone. We all have to ask for forgiveness, so we must learn to forgive others if we want to be forgiven ourselves.

We need to forgive ourselves. There are decisions that we have made that have hurt others. No one is immune from hurting people. We can be our worst enemy. When we can not forgive ourselves for some offense, we hinder our own lives. We punish ourselves in many ways. Some people say that they don't deserve love or happiness because of an offense they committed. I do believe that whenever possible you should make amends for what you have done; however, some things can't be fixed or corrected. Forgive yourself for the action and move on with your life. If you need to call someone or write a letter to them asking for forgiveness, do it. You can't control how they will respond. Your goal is to free them and yourself.

Forgiving also means to stop the offense. You can't say you have forgiven someone if they are continuing to hurt you in the same manner. Forgiveness isn't being weak or complacent. You have a right to be safe, respected and not abused in any manner. You have to stand up for yourself whenever you can. You have to advocate for yourself. I have worked with people who are child advocates. Their job is to act in the best interest of the children in a situation, because the children are unable to protect themselves.

As parents we must protect our children. Don't allow them to grow up in fear because they were abused or neglected in some manner. Be aware of the people you allow into your childrens' lives. If they continually don't want to be around someone, you must find out why. Children don't usually lie about being abused. We must address this epidemic of child abuse in our society. I totally believe in forgiving the person, but the offense must end. Your child must be safe.

If you were abused in your past, identify with it and let it go. If you need outside counseling and support, get it. Don't be ashamed of something you couldn't control as a child. Take control now and forgive that person and heal yourself. Negativity can kill people. It can destroy your spirit and rob you of joy and peace. Again, I am not suggesting that you continue to allow someone who hurt you to be in your life. Forgiveness means not holding on to the wrong done to you. It may not be healthy to be around someone who abused or hurt you deeply. Wisdom is required to forgive someone and decide if they are going to be a part of your life. That person needs to get help for themselves, because hurting people hurt other people. It is a sad thing to find out that someone died who you had a grudge against that could have been rectified.

Words are powerful but they can also heal a situation when they once deeply hurt someone. The words, "I'm sorry," when heartfelt, can go a long way. Again, I'm not telling you to put yourself or others you love in unsafe or unhealthy situations or relationships. Forgive them and go on with your life in a positive direction. You will be a stronger person.

You have a right to be angry when you were violated or hurt, but you must learn to forgive them and enjoy life in a healthy way.

If you are in an unhealthy relationship right now, end it! You know that it's unhealthy when you are unhappy and a voice inside you tells you that something is wrong. Listen to that voice. I believe that God gives us all warnings that we are in danger. Pay attention to it. Some call it intuition, others call it insight. Whatever you call it, don't tune it out. We have all had experiences where we didn't listen to our inner voice and we regretted it later. If you're unsure if you are in an unhealthy situation, ask someone you trust. I have a test I use when I have a decision to make and I'm unsure of what to do. I make a list of pros and cons and see which list is bigger. If the pros outweigh the cons, but you are still unhappy, re-evaluate your list and again seek the advice of someone who will tell you the truth. They must be a wise, trustworthy person. Listen to them, but, more important, listen to yourself. The signals we receive are warning us to do something different and check out what is wrong.

To any young person reading this, If you are being abused, mistreated or made to feel like you have to do things that are inappropriate or make you feel bad, tell someone. Even if it is a family member, teacher, coach or some other person you respect. Talk until someone listens to you. You are very valuable and you have every right to feel safe as a teenager. Seek help. Talk to someone today, and don't feel bad about it. It's not your fault. I'll repeat that. It's not your fault! You must love yourself enough to seek help. A telephone operator can give you anonymous phone numbers to call if you can't trust anyone you know. Whatever you do, don't give up hope. Help is available.

When you forgive, you empower yourself and you gain so much. You gain control over your life, thoughts and actions. You control your destiny. You can have healthy relationships with people. You release negative energy from the atmosphere and replace it with positive energy.

You are happier and healthier. You are not weighed down with hurt, sorrow and negativity. It is a challenge but it is beautiful to forgive yourself and others. Try it. I urge you to release any pain, misery and unhappiness from your past. Let it go and you'll reap the benefits and freedom that forgiveness brings and truly enjoy life.

Exhibiting Excellence is Beautiful

The last character of beauty I will discuss is excellence. Exhibiting excellence means going above and beyond that which is normal and/or expected. People who utilize this character are very motivated, driven, and are very successful. They work longer hours than most people. They don't give up when facing a challenge. Challenges encourage them to overcome them and do better. They tend to work well under pressure and have deadlines to accomplish their goals. They sacrifice a lot and they are often misunderstood or judged by others because of their dedication and commitment. Mediocrity is not a part of their vocabulary. They aim high, shoot for the moon and work until they achieve their goals. They quickly move on to a new goal. They have short and long range plans. They achieve great things. Some people call them movers and shakers. They don't take no for an answer. They open doors for themselves and they surround themselves with like-minded people. They often lose relationships, because as they achieve more and go to a higher level, their previous relationships don't tend to relate to them anymore.

I do caution you if you are a person of excellence. Excellence is not arrogance. It is not stepping on the backs and necks of others to get what you desire. It is not hurting people, being malicious, self-seeking or lacking in compassion. Excellence is being driven to succeed. If you are truly excellent, you will remember where you came from and you will help others as you excel. They may not always understand and agree with you, but you have the ability to help make the world a better place. Always be gracious and humble. No man is an island. You received help from someone in some way. Maybe it was a book you read or a conversation you overheard that motivated you. Maybe it was your childhood struggles that you had to overcome. Maybe you are diligent about working hard because you were taught to have a good work ethic. Whatever motivated you to excel, give credit to it or those people. That experience helped you become the success that you are.

Excellence doesn't mean instant success. It is a battle. It is a process. People who exhibit excellence aren't perfect. They make mistakes; lose money, time and sometimes relationships. What do you value? If a relationship is suffering because of your goals, evaluate if it is worth it. Don't underestimate yourself and the power that God has given you. We need people of excellence in the world to help pave the way for others to follow.

God Made Me Beautiful, But I Didn't Know It

Melissa Boston is a personal example of being excellent. She is a top leader in the fast growing travel industry. She has hundreds of people under her leadership in less than a three-year period. She travels around the country giving presentations, coaching assistance and has weekly meetings and conference calls. She is a trend setter. She recently gave up her corporate job to work fulltime with her home-based business. She works to build her team and she has a wealth of information that she readily shares to anyone interested. She also has a warm down-to- earth and drawing presence. She is a woman of excellence.

When excellence is exhibited, true dedication is required. No half stepping or sloppy work, shortcuts or cutting of corners is accepted. No excuses are accepted. No mountain is too high to climb. If it can't be climbed, then a person of excellence goes around or through the mountain.

People of excellence are often history makers. Harriet Tubman freed hundreds of slaves because she was a woman of excellence. She didn't allow being a slave, a woman or even having a medical condition stop her from freeing people. She was a woman with a purpose as well as a woman of excellence. Martin Luther King Jr., Malcom X, Nelson Mandela, Muhammad Ali, Oprah Winfrey, Magic Johnson, Tyler Perry and Bill Gates are all examples of people of excellence. Their contributions to society are known around the world. Muhammad Ali was even called "the greatest" because of his record in boxing at that time. There are far too many other people of excellence to list, but one thing people of excellence have in common is their commitment to fulfill their goal and that makes them beautiful.

I have chosen these sixteen characteristics of beauty because they are essential traits that we all have in some capacity. Some of the traits we are strong in and some we are weak in. The stronger traits are obvious to other people and hopefully after reading this book you are now familiar with your own strong character traits of beauty. We can all work on improving our weak traits. It may mean looking deep inside ourselves to find these traits that are hidden or covered by the scars of life. I do encourage you to work on healing those scars.

There are some other traits of beauty which I want to briefly mention. Creativity, imagination, leadership, compassion, respect, courage and organization are some of them. These traits are also helpful to our society.

Everything begins in your mind with a simple thought. Your thoughts will become words and then actions. Guard your mind. Read positive literature and books. Talk to positive people. Affirm yourself on a daily basis. Visualize your dreams frequently. This will put your subconscious mind to work. What you constantly think about will materialize in the real world. If you want to be happy and successful, you must work hard and surround yourself with people that will support your dreams. Let go of any negativity from your past and present.

You are beautiful. I truly believe that God made us all and, therefore, we are special and beautiful. I hope this book encourages you to recognize what true beauty is and that you will put that beauty to work today. I have a deep love and passion in my heart to see people enjoy life. If

I can be a servant, conduit or an oracle to help you see your beauty in any way, then I have fulfilled my purpose. Beauty is a part of you. It is your nature. I wish you light, peace and blessings as you persevere through your life.

Epilogue

When I first started writing this book, I had a different outline planned. I planned on writing this book with support from a group of women, but it turned out that this book was truly my vision. I am aware that my friends and family do support and care for me, but this book was something I had to write on my own. It is my legacy and my passion, not theirs. I had to use my own words. At times I felt discouraged and felt like I didn't have enough words to say, but looking back I see how it's all come together. It's just God. I have a wrist band that I wear daily. It says, "Just God." It's a positive affirmation from my church. We are wearing it for the whole year of 2007. I look at it daily and it reminds me that I am not in control of everything, but it is God who opens doors for me. My part is to be faithful, work hard and be purpose-driven, thankful and encouraging to others and the rest of the things I need will be manifested in my life. I believe that you reap what you sow and I pray that this book will sow all of the characteristics of beauty in your life as you read this book.

Recently I watched a TV program that was called Monique's FAT Chance. FAT stands for fabulous and thick. The show was about full- figured women competing in a modeling contest in Paris. In actuality, the show was so much more. The five women all won because of their attitude change about themselves. Monique helped them find their inner beauty and learn to love and embrace their bodies now. She helped them see their true beauty is not based on the size and shape of their body, but on their heart and strengths. I loved it. Not to mention, they were able to enjoy a visit to Paris as well as improve their self-esteem. I truly respect Monique for what she has done for so many women who look down on themselves because they are not considered to be beautiful because of their size.

There are several songs about beauty out now. I really enjoy these songs. India Arie sings about her beauty not being about what she wears, looks like or some super model description of beauty. She is aware that beauty is internal a spiritual thing, and she is beautiful and her songs express that beauty to others.

Beauty is what you are, not just some physical dimension. It's the total package of what makes each person unique and whole. We must learn how to embrace ourselves with love, which is the most important character of beauty. If we love ourselves, then we can love others and the world will be a better place for all of us to live in. Find and enjoy your beauty!